Contents

Making Music

Plucking

Angela Aylmore

Heinemann
LIBRARY

Little Nippers

www.heinemann.co.uk/library
Visit our website to find out more information about Heinemann Library books.

To order:
☎ Phone 44 (0) 1865 888066
📠 Send a fax to 44 (0) 1865 314091
💻 Visit the Heinemann Bookshop at www.heinemann.co.uk/library to browse our catalogue and order online.

First published in Great Britain by Heinemann Library, Halley Court, Jordan Hill, Oxford OX2 8EJ, part of Harcourt Education.

Heinemann is a registered trademark of Harcourt Education Ltd.

© Harcourt Education Ltd 2005.
First published in paperback in 2005.
The moral right of the proprietor has been asserted.

Editorial: Kathy Peltan and Kate Bellamy
Design: Jo Hinton-Malivoire and Bigtop
Picture Research: Ruth Blair
Production: Severine Ribierre

Originated by Chroma Graphics (Overseas) Pte Ltd.
Printed and bound in China by South China Printing Company

ISBN 0 431 08823 3 (hardback)
09 08 07 06 05
10 9 8 7 6 5 4 3 2 1

ISBN 0 431 08828 4 (paperback)
09 08 07 06 05
10 9 8 7 6 5 4 3 2 1

British Library Cataloguing in Publication Data
Aylmore, Angela
Making Music: Plucking
787.8
A full catalogue record for this book is available from the British Library.

Acknowledgements
The publishers would like to thank the following for permission to reproduce photographs: Alamy pp. **4b**, **5a**, **12**, **17**, **18**; Corbis pp. **4a**, **5b**; Getty Images p. **19** (Photodisc); Harcourt Education pp. **14**, **15** (Gareth Boden); **13** (Debbie Rowe); **6**, **7**, **8**, **9**, **10a**, **10b**, **11**, **16**, **20**, **21**, **22-23** (Tudor Photography).

Cover photograph of a girl playing a guitar, reproduced with permission of Alamy.

Every effort has been made to contact copyright holders of any material reproduced in this book. Any omissions will be rectified in subsequent printings if notice is given to the publishers.

The paper used to print this book comes from sustainable resources.

Listen to the lap harp.

Use all of your fingers to play the harp.

Pling, bling

Fingers and thumbs

Put your finger on the string.
Now pluck it!

pluck

Move your fingers quickly. How **fast** can they go?

pluck
pluck
pluck
pluck
pluck

Pluck the guitar

Can you play
the guitar?

Pluck it gently.
Make a soft note.

Pluck it hard.
Make a **loud** note.

Big and small

Listen to the **big** cello.

Listen to the small violin.

Up tall or down flat?

This harp stands up tall.

I sit next to it to play it.

This harp lies
down flat.

I play it on
my lap.

Make your own

Can you make an instrument to pluck?

Use a box and some rubber bands.

twang-g-g

Pluck the rubber bands
to make a note.

Sounds like...

Pluck some notes on a violin.

What does it sound like?

Does it make you think of a dripping tap?

What is it?

This is a sitar. It comes from India.

This part of the
sitar is round.
It is made from
a pumpkin.

Listen carefully

What can you hear?
What makes that sound?

violin

maracas

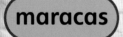

recorder

triangle

It's the violin!

21

All together now!

23

Index

Notes for adults

Making Music provides children with an opportunity to think about sound and the different ways instruments can be played to create music. The concept of volume, rhythm, speed and pitch are introduced, and children are encouraged to think about how controlling their movements can create different sounds when they play instruments. The following Early Learning Goals are relevant to this series:

Creative development - music
• explore the different sounds of instruments and learn how sounds can be changed

Knowledge and understanding of the world
• look closely at similarities, differences, patterns and change
• show an interest in why things happen and how things work

Physical development
• respond to rhythm by means of gesture and movement
• manage body to create intended movements

This book looks at how to creating music by plucking. It looks at different instruments, large and small, that have strings, and the type of sound they make. Plucking is a good way for children to practice control over some complex motor-skills, as the book demonstrates how to pluck to make quick, slow, loud and soft sounds.

Follow-up activities

• Demonstrate to the children how plucking different sized strings on a stringed instrument can produce different notes. Pluck a thick string to produce a low note and a thin string to produce a high note.

• instruments can be used as links into history topics. An example of an historical stringed instrument is the lyre, which was used by the Ancient Greeks. Show the children pictures of a lyre and ask them if they think it looks like any of the instruments they have seen in this book. What do they think it would have sounded like?